John Gillette's inspirational book *Glorify God* is a fantastic reminder of how I should approach each day and how blessed I am. It is so easy to get caught up in the hustle and bustle of today's lifestyle and forget what is really important. John's encouraging words are a great reminder of how we all should live each day. I have a great foundation of faith nut John's book helps me to remember what is important and allows me to reflect on the wonderful things I have and to be gracious to God for those blessings.

— *Tammy Thelen, Au.D., CCC-A*

I0460858

Note from the Author

I believe in God's sovereignty and compassion. I am learning to let go of self and to hold onto someone that can do whatever he pleases. Sometimes life is cruel, sometimes it is full of suffering, physically and psychologically. A spiritual solution to meet difficult trials has become my goal. God's Word carries with it no uncertainties. I want it to saturate my mind and heart..

The *Pastoral Health Care Series* and *Divine Dialogue Series* was created through unexpected heart disease (open heart surgery), cancer (medication and surgery), a stroke and major head injury after a car accident that also resulted in the death of my wife.

It is helping me to develop and adequate level to supernatural, psychological and physical adjustments. It may help you as well. It has brought me security.

—*John F. Gillette, Ph.D., D.Min*

DISCOVERING

GOD'S

Infinite
Nature

John Gillette's writings flow from a lifetime of experience. It is one thing to write out of a knowledge based on research. It is an entirely different thing to write out of a depth of life experience. John has both. As a pastor who has cared for the needs of a congregation, as a husband who has experienced the tragic loss of a wife, and as a child of God who has walked through the joys and pain of following the Lord, John has so much to offer in this series. From the opening pages, through to the very end, you will be blessed by the insights, loving tone and encouragement you receive from this series. God has used John greatly in ministry and will continue to use him through this life-giving series.

—*Josh Mateer, D. Min.*

True, illustrative, practical stories are like windows that unlock Bible truths and promises. Along with a masterfully orchestrated short stories should come the truth that God's Word and love has been experienced by His servants as they partner with Him in the work of rebuilding the Kingdom. A gifted teacher, Dr. Gillette lives an ordinary life abiding in Christ and being an obedient servant of the Lord. As he sees God working in his life, and in the lives of those to whom he ministers, his faith is refreshed and he is encouraged to press on through life's uncertainties.

Only a lifetime dedicated to nurturing, ministering, teaching, and keen insight through the power of the Holy Spirit, can produce such poignant stories that teach and challenge.

—*Mulonge M. Kalumbula, Ph.D.*

John's books give us hope and light. He reminds us that through Jesus we are never alone. I have certainly needed that reminder in my life and in my practice. In holding a patient's hand, and helping them through a condition or disease, reminding them that they are never alone has become the greatest gift of health care.

—*Linda M. Kunce, D.C.*

The series reminds me that Jesus knows what it's like to live in a human body. I have received Jesus and His forgiveness, but as the book suggests, I also have the power from the Holy Spirit. His books have encouraged me to gain courage through prayer and confidence in Jesus to meet my needs. John's honesty is very special to read as he reflects on his own life and struggles. I like his explanation that "the soul is where the emotions are and the mind is where the thinking takes place". It's been good for me to read that God works through weakness, and learn that John found God with him in the middle of the struggles.

—*Arvid W. Vandyke, Ed.D.*

Discovering God's Counsel is a book full of great spiritual truths from someone who has developed a very close and deep relationship with Jesus through his life. John provides a meaningful and inspirational testimony, with examples from his own experiences, of how relying on God's Word and promises can give you the power, hope, and peace you need to overcome life's struggles and challenges. The Scriptures he chose in his book were on point and helpful. It was an enjoyable and wonderful read.

—*Thoa Reyna, J.D.*

John has written a user-friendly and practical series for anyone desiring to live beyond the superficial and venture into the supernatural. The world needs this *Pastoral Health Care Series*. Pastors and followers of Jesus need the insights from John's lifetime experience of walking with God and caring for His people through the power of the Holy Spirit. John has brilliantly show that God is enough, God's love is real, God's counsel is enduring, and God reigns supremely. This important series will serve both the church and the world for many years to come.

—*Kizombo Kalumbula, Jr., Ph.D.*

FANTASTIC
FAVORITES
PART 5

DISCOVERING

GOD'S

Infinite

Nature

Who has brought me to an
in-depth study of God . . . Jesus Christ?

JOHN F. GILLETTE

Chapbook Press
Schuler Books
2660 28th Street SE
Grand Rapids MI 49512

www.schulerbooks.com/chapbook-press

Fantastic Favorites Book Series Part Five
Discovering God's Infinite Nature: Who has brought me to an in-depth study of God . . . Jesus Christ?
Copyright ©2024 — John F. Gillette. All rights reserved. Published 2024.

Printed at Schuler Books, Chapbook Press, Grand Rapids, Michigan, in the United States of America.

Distribution contact:at jjgillette@comcast.net.

ISBN 13: 9781966196075

Library of Congress Control Number: 2024925533

Cover photo: Paige Weber/Unsplash
Cover Design: Frank Gutbrod Graphic Design

Printed in the United States of America

Books by John Gillette:

Pastoral Health Care

Discovering God's Sufficiency
Going Beyond Ourselves and Experiencing the Supernatural
Part One

Discovering God's Love
Confirming God's Love Through the Evidence of Historical Facts
Part Two

Discovering God's Counsel
Applying His Spiritual Solution to Meet Difficult Trials
Part Three

Discovering God's Kingdom
Finding a Way to Understand Ourselves in a Complex World
Part Four

Discovering God's Heart
Finding God's Heart Pulse is Our Daily Challenge
Part Five

Divine Dialogue

Glorify God
Christianity is a Divine Vitality
Part One

Dynamic Doer
Biblical Christianity is Jesus Christ
Part Two

Satisfying Strength
Biblical Meditation Works — Allow Psalms to Sweep You into All Directions
Part Three

Disciplining Dynamics
Christian Counseling Teaching Tools
Part Four

Celebrate Christ
Above All Christ
Part Five

Fantastic Favorites

Discovering God's Presence
What does it mean to live in Jesus Christ?
Part One

Discovering God's Grace
What does it mean to magnify Jesus Christ?
Part Two

Discovering God's Supernatural Activities
Why Do I Believe in Jesus Christ?
Part Three

Discovering God's Intimacy
How should I talk to Jesus Christ?
Part Four

Discovering God's Infinite Nature
Who has brought me to an in-depth study of God . . . Jesus Christ?
Part Five

Joy and John Gillette

It is with great affection that I dedicate this book series to my wife, Joy, who radiates God's grace. We wrote the pastoral health care series together. Applying God's spiritual solutions to meet us in difficult trials has become even more practical in my life with the death of my dear wife, Joy. This book has been reproduced in her memory. While the content is the same, my dedication has become more personal than ever before. The separation is painful but as I gather my suffering and feeling of incompleteness, I will succeed with God's peace and presence. The guidelines of this book have brought blessing to our life together. We have pursued them with great persistence. I am assured that she is in God's presence, rejoicing and at peace. I will be with her to experience God's eternal presence someday as well.

". . . blessed are they who put their trust in Him."

Table of Contents

Introduction

God's infinite nature refers to the Almighty Supreme Being. It emphasizes the inexhaustible attributes. He is without limits. He is all knowing, all powerful and all loving. It deals with the essence of God's character. The book was written to understand and accept God's will in the tragic loss of my wife Joy. In the physical and Ps.ychological pain, I need to experience God's love, faith and hope. The pain caused passion to create a holy urge. I am not content with earthly reasons. It is a deep desire to integrate love, faith and hope in the inner self. It is a touch of God's infinite nature to cause peace. It is Jesus Christ for me (grace), it is Christ in me (faith) and Christ through me (work). Travel with me in reading my book and you will discover and understand through personal decision, biblical saturation, divine attributes, angelic beings, human creation, Jesus Christ involvement , the body of Christ, future events, the Holy Spirit involvement and personal involvement. Strength, steadfastness, satisfaction, saturation will slowly settle into place in the spirit, soul and body. Love is the motivation behind my life. It is self-giving. I have experienced God's affection. Faith is the foundation of my life. It is reliable. I have trusted him. He has been steadfast. Hope includes the others together with expectation in my life. The gateway is found through the Holy Spirit "Be filled with the spirit" Eph 5:18.

God's Infinite Nature is understood through Personal Decision

The decision is to "seek God" (Matt. 6:23). Seeking is a deep desire to delight in his counsel. "Blessed is the man that walketh not in the counsel of the ungodly but his delight is in the law of the Lord: and in his law does he meditate day and night (Ps. 11:1-2). The word blessed relates to happiness, this produces a firm foundation, passion, knowledge and patience. I thank God for giving me christian parents that produced a firm foundation. I grew up with a passion for the Bible.

Absolute knowledge has its foundation on God's intellect. Law gives conviction, courage and challenge. I believe in Almighty God.

- Delight means that I enjoy the word.
- Law means instruction is found in scripture.
- Meditation means to ponder over the Bible.
- Happiness will be a solid result.

Seeking leads to trust. "In thee Lord I put my trust" (Ps. 11:1) "Trusting is putting my confidence in a thought or person (Ps. 119:44). "My heart shall rejoice in Jesus Christ because I have trusted" (Ps. 33:21). I trust in deliverance (Ps. 22). I trust in guidance (Ps. 31). I trust in providence (Ps. 23). I trust in safety (Ps. 56). Trust leads to belief. My life is based on God's perspective not emotions or circumstances. Seeking, trusting, believing are decisions made with God's infinite nature.

- God is faithful (my doubt)
- God is holy (my sinfulness)
- God is love (my selfishness)
- God is truth (falsehood)
- God is absolute knowledge (my questioning)
- God is all powerful (my fear)

- God is everywhere (my presents)
- God is Lord (my disobedience)

God's infinite nature is understood through personal decision.

God's Infinite Nature is understood through Biblical Saturation

The study of God's Infinite Nature is theology. Theology is a compound of two Greek words (theos-God) and (Logos-speech of expression). Both Christ as the living word and the Bible as the written word are the Logos of God (John 1:1). God's presence, power and purpose is our topic (Rom. 3:2; 1 Peter 4:11; Luke 8:21).

The Bible is the sole rule of faith and practice. It's the only dependable source of information. The scriptures are the Oracles of God. The finite mind is limited to the infinite revelation. The only way to understand is through spiritual illumination (Luke 24:27) The surrender to the will and mind of God is essential (Rom. 8:14; 1 Cor. 2:15). It is a life undertaking (2 Tim. 2:15). It will take faith to respond (1 Cor. 2:14; 1 Cor. 3:1-3; Heb. 11:3; John 7:17; 1 Cor. 2:15; 1 John 2:27).

The orthodox view of the Bible is the infallible word of God. Human reason and knowledge must be reliant on the scriptures. The scripture (alone) is authority. Rational view denies any divine revelation (Luke 18:8; 2 Tim. 3:13). The word alone deals with things eternal and infinite; it alone has power to convert the soul and to develop a God honoring the spiritual life (1 Thes. 2:13-14). Biblical saturation can be secure through daily study of scripture. The Bible in its original writing is the inerrant word of God it is called sacred scripture by way of eminence (John 7:42; 5:39; 2 John 3:15). God's word is perfect (Prov. 30:5; Ps. 19:7; Ps. 18:30). God's infinite nature is understood through Biblical saturation.

God's Infinite Nature was understood through Biblical saturation. I discovered that Jesus Christ is the living word and the Bible is the written word and the logos of God. The Bible became my rule of faith and practice. It is the only dependable source of belief. The only way to understand is through spiritual illumination.

THREE

God's infinite nature is understood through Divine Attributes

God's attributes reveal his character as a person, holiness is the most important attribute because it defines everything else. Holiness is defined as being separate or set apart from everything that is not God. We stand in awe because of God's intellect. To <u>stand</u> in awe (Ps. 3:4) is reverential respect mixed with fear and wonder. We <u>kneel</u> before God because of his depth of wisdom and knowledge (Rom. 11:33). We <u>weep</u> because of your work on our behalf (Ps. 92:5). We are <u>humble</u> because God knows us (Ps. 139:1). He is sensitive. He has sensibility. God Knows our feelings.

- It involves holiness: darkness-light (John 1:4-5)
- It involves justice: believe-righteous (Rom. 3:26)
- It involves love: reconcile-impute (2 Cor. 5:19)
- It involves truth: promise-faithful (Heb. 10:23)

The word involve means to participate. Look up each word and decide the difference. Do something about it !

He acts with wisdom and power.

God is able to do whatever he will. His attributes acts with:

- Infinity — endlessness — to big to measure
- Sovereignty — supreme power — complete authority
- Glory — honor God's greatness and splendor

We see God the one inner essences with their promise.

- God the Father
- God the Son
- God the Holy Spirit.

God's infinite nature is understood through divine attributes

FOUR

God's infinite nature is understood through Angelic Beings

Celestial beings are angels. The word angel means messenger. The sacred scripture does imply that angels may have bodies.

- It is recorded at creation.
- It was given with the law.
- It was at the birth of christ.
- It was recorded at the temptations.
- It was at the resurrection.
- It was at the ascension.
- It will be at the second coming.

They serve God and fulfill his purpose. They hold official positions. They represent God. They defend God. They worship God. They exalt God. They are spirit-messengers. They are subordinate to christ. Satan was an angel he was condemned for his pride of hate (1 Tim 3:6). He goes from place to place (Job 1:6-12; 2:1-7; Matt. 4:10,11; Mark 4:15). He is a celestial and territorial ruler (Eph. 2:2; 6:10-18; 2 Cor. 4:4; John 12:31). He has a realm divided into organized principalities and is the head of all the powers of darkness and ignorance (Daniel 10:12-11; Matt. 12:24-30; Eph. 6:10-12). He controls fallen angels and fallen men (Matt. 25:41; John 8:44; James 2:19; 1 John 3:8-10; Rev. 12:5). He is active in some religions and religious affairs (2 Cor. 11:14; Rev. 2:9; 3:9). He sows tare among the wheat, and is the enemy and accuser of the church (1 Peter 5:8; Rev. 12:5). He is the author of persecution and tribulation, and afflicts the bodies of the men (Luke 13:16; Acts 10:38; 1 Cor. 5:5; 2 Cor. 12:1-8; 1 Tim. 1:20; Rev. 2:10). He attacks with cunning snares and with fiery darts, and suggests evil thought (John 13:2; Acts 5:3; 1 Cor. 7:5; 2 Cor. 2:11; 11:4; Eph. 4:27; 1 Tim. 3:7; 6:7; 2 Tim. 2:26; Eph. 6:16). He has power over man extending to death, but not beyond it (Heb. 2:14)

He has overcome by christ (Luke 10:18; Acts 26:18; Heb. 2:14; 1 John 3:8), and can be successfully resisted by the christian (Rom. 16:20; 6:11; James 4:7; 1 Peter 5:9; 1 John 2:13; 5:18; Rev. 12:11). He will share the eternal doom of all those whom he has seduced (Rev. 20:1-3; 7-15). Our responsibility regarding Satan is clear we must be sober and watch, lest he devours us (1 Peter 5:8,9). We must give him no foothold whatever (Eph. 4:27) we must resist him in virtue of the cross (James 4:7; 1 Peter 5:8,9). We must put on whole armor of God (Eph. 6:11-18). We must not be ignorant of his crafty devices (2 Cor. 2:11) we must overcome him by the victorious word (Matt. 4:1-11; 1 John 2:14). We must triumph overcome him in Christ's name (Eph. 1:19-22; 2:6; 2 Cor. 2:15). We must overcome him by the Holy Spirit (Rom. 8:1-13; Gal. 5:15-26). We must overcome him by regeneration and faith (1 John 2:29; 3:9; 5:1-4,18). We must overcome him by the blood of Christ and our testimony (Rev. 12:11). Satan is a defeated foe. The lord Jesus spoke of Satan and demons as living beings, just as real as himself. He claimed that his binding of Satan and casting out of demons by the spirit of God was proof that he was God and Messiah (Matt. 12:22-29). When the disciples could not cast out demons, Jesus ordered the "deaf and dumb spirit" to come out and the boy was healed. Later Jesus privately explained the problem. "this kind can come forth by nothing, but by prayer and fasting" (Mark 9:29). He did not tell them that the problem was only Psychosomatic and that they needed the power of positive thinking! Satan and demons may be invisible, but according to Christ and the Bible, they are real, personal spirit beings who are enemies of God and mankind, especially of God's children. All the New testament writers (though not every book) mention Satan and demons. We can be assured that the Son of God, who personally confronted Satan (Matt. 4:1-11) and demons (Luke 8:26-39), know the truth of their reality and power. He spoke and acted in accord with truth in defeating them.

The best Biblical evidence supports that demons are fallen angels. When Lucifer, the highest ranking angelic cherub, rebelled against God in his desire to be like the most high and rule over men and angels, he carried with him an army of followers, probably a third of all angels who became demons (Rev. 12:3-7). Lucifer (Heb., "the shining one") became Satan (Heb., "opposer"). His corruption and his powers perverted.

In scripture the term spirit is always used in reference to personal beings. Demons have intellect , emotion, and will. In other words, they have personality. Demons have supernatural intelligence and strength which are sometimes used to control men (Acts 19:16; Mark 5:3). They are not restricted by physical barriers as men are.Demons are Satan's untiring and devoted henchmen, organized to accomplish their common purpose of opposing God's program. They promote the philosophy of creaturecenteredness in individuals, in governments, and in the world system (1 John 2:15-17; John 12:31). Demons promote a philosophy that denies the creation and judgment of moral absolutes, thus opening humans to all they promote rebellion against God's character and encourage men to blame God for restrictions and for the existence of evil and suffering (Rev. 16:9,11; 18;8-10). They accuse men before God, as does Satan, and often cause condemning thoughts, even when Christ has already brought forgiveness (1 John 1:9; 2:1-2). Demons promote false religions and cults. They are the dynamic force behind idolatry (Ps. 96:4-5; 106:36-38), receiving the worship of evil spirits involved, to the spirits the idols represent. The false religions where magic, superstition, and worship of evil spirits are involved, demons actually intervene to encourage their devotees and lead them into further bondage (1 Cor. 12:1-3; Acts 8:9-11). Satan and demons particularly abhor God's grace in Christ. They cannot repent and be saved, and they prevent others from doing so. They deny and distort God's grace in salvation and lead men to denial of sin or the works-righteousness religions, even twisting the purpose of God by "bewitching" through false teachers (Gal. 2:21-3:1). They move men to apostatize from the truth in Christ and to adhere to demonic teachers.

But their actions extend even beyond perpetrating lies that eventually lead people to hell. Demons also distress men here and now. They may cause natural catastrophes, degrade man's nature, disable the body with dumbness, blindness, deformity, and disease. They may drive a person to insanity or promate suicidal mania and injury (Luke 8:27, 13,24; Mark 9:22; 5:5; Luke 9:39). They may move men to harm and destroy human life and bring men and women into slavery and sexual perversion (Rom. 1:18-32; Rev. 18:2,13,24). In the Bible and in secular history and culture, idolatry and immorality are always connected.

Demons may do to believers much of what they do to unbelievers. The believers are eternally secure in the grace of salvation (Rom. 8:38-39). However, the battle here and now has its dangers. We do not wrestle merely with humans in opposition to the gospel and to godly living, but against the Devil, his henchmen, and their schemes (Eph. 6:10-18). Though much of our struggle against sin comes from our own sinful nature (Rom. 7:21-24; James 1:14-15), we must recognize the possibility of demonic attacks personally or corporately as a church. We cannot as christians true to God's word, dismiss the possibility of demonic affliction. Demons attack confidence in God's word, God's love and goodness, and seek to destroy commitment to christ. They may create divisions within the church by false doctrine, bad lifestyles, faulty leadership, and worldly philosophy of ministry (1 Tim. 4:1-3; Jude 4; Rev. 2:20-24; Col. 2:16-22; 1 Tim. 3:5-9; 6:3-10).

Opposition to evangelizing and discipling efforts come from demons and the men they use. They may incite persecution and seek our death. Some men in following them may actually think they are serving God (John 16:1-3). While God may overrule demonic activity to correct defection

(1 Sam. 1:19-20; 1 Cor. 5:5), create discernment (Job 40:1-4; 42:1-6), cultivate dependence (2 Cor. 12:7-10),or arouse to battle (Eph. 6:10-18).

There are many tricksters who represent themselves as being involved in the occult. But this fact should not blind us to actual demonic activities. God warned Israel by Moses against the spiritism of magicians who had the power to duplicate divine miracles (Exod. 7:8-13). Antichrist will perform false signs and wonders during the time of tribulation at the end of this age (2 Thess. 2:8-9). Christians ought not to be deceived by fortune-tellers. They may be demon energized and confirmed by the conspiracies of Satan and his host (Acts 16:16-19). Astrology, laying of cards, palm reading, rod and pendulum, water witching, ESP, and certain dreams and visions are used by demons to turn men from depending upon God and to seeking personal advantage by forbidden knowledge and power. When Saul sought Samuel's spirit by the medium of endor, he was judged by God (1 Sam. 28:3.9; 1 Chron. 10:13-14).occult practices may result in demonic oppression and, frequently, inhabitation. God may allow this as part of the judgment upon idolatrous practices (Exod. 20:4-6; Rom. 1:18-32).

The term possession is a misleading translation, picturing someone under total control, wild and violent, or maliciously evil. That is not the picture of many in the new testament. In some cases, they seemed afflicted by illness and not altogether opposed to God and the truth. Furthermore, demons do not possess or own anything. God owns them. They are His creatures and he is their judge. If they inhabit a person, they have only squatter's rights. They violate God's laws of the sanctity of the person and his body (1 Cor. 6:13). The term demonized better reflects the Greek daimonizomai (Matt. 15:22), literally a state of demon caused passivity. Practically, it refers to the condition of a person who is controlled more or less in various ways by inhabiting demons. Its equivalent is to have a demon (Mark 1:23; 9:17; Acts 8:7).

The lord Jesus described this reality of spirit inhabiting and affecting a person (Matt. 12:22-28) and claiming the person's body as his residence (Matt. 12:43-45). We cannot, as honest, thinking, christian, believe the Bible and christ, and deny the phenomenon of demonization.

Symptoms may seem to overlap with certain mental, emotional, or physical disorders, as they did on the gospels. But symptoms such as unusual physical strength or intelligence, sudden changes and reverses in emotions, manifestation of another personality, continual blasphemous thoughts, and recurrent urges to harm or to commit suicide must be considered as possibly demonic in estimating a person's condition (see Matt. 5:1-20). Inability to trust God, pray, read the Bible, say the name of the Lord Jesus, and resistance to spiritual truth are even more suspicious symptoms. So also the appearance of dark figures. Mediumistic or clairvoyant powers. Falling into trances, change of persons speaking, magical abilities, inserted or unwanted thoughts, and voices that attack God or the person all point in the direction of demonic activity.

God's Infinite Nature was understood through angelic beings. They are messengers from God. Angels serve God and fulfill his purpose. Satan and demons are fallen angels. We have victory by putting on the armor of God (Eph. 6:4-18).

God's infinite nature is understood through Human Creation

The Bible says "know ye that the Lord he is God; it is he that hath made us and not ourselves; we are his people and the sheep of his pasture" (Ps. 100:3). We have a God who is our creator and Lord and one who does decide and manage our destiny.

A lot of students become convinced that the theory of evolution is a proven scientific fact because almost all biology books—highschool and collage—include evidence that weakens theory. Therefore, their minds have been made up before they consider the evidence. They feel that the theory of evolution must be true because they cannot believe that God has created living things—"In the beginning God created the heaven and the earth." (Gen. 1:1). They believe it is unscientific to believe in the only alternative—special creation.

What it boils down to is simply faith in man's authority or faith in God's authority. An important difference between the creationist and the evolutionist is that the creationist admits that he has faith, while the evolutionist denies that faith has anything to do with his acceptance of the theory of evolution.

The reason that most scientists accept the theory of evolution is that they are unbelievers and unbelieving materialistic men are forced to accept a materialistic, naturalistic, explanation for the origin of all living things.

There are only two possible ways to explain the origin of living things. Either living things arose by a naturalistic process of evolution or they were created. If one refuses to accept the fact that God exists, a God who created heaven and the earth, then to that person evolution becomes a fact.

Evolution is a hypothesis, a scientific idea or guess not a fact.

The Bible is God's revelation to man. We know that God exists because he has been revealed to us through his son, the Lord Jesus Christ, our risen living savior. Let us never abandon the Authority of the Holy Scriptures in favor of men's authority.

God hath made us (Ps. 100:3)—"In the beginning God created heaven and the earth". (Gen 1:1). This is a description in broad outline of the creative acts of God which brought into being all living things. Man is threefold—(may the God of peace himself sanctify you entirely; and may your spirit and soul and body be preserved complete, without blame at the coming of our Lord Jesus Christ." (1 Thess. 5:23).

Man is spirit because he is dependent upon God. This is the nucleus of life; the life principle; the source of life: God-conscious; worshipful part of man; likeness of God. the inbreathing of God was an endless life not subject to death "and the Lord God formed man of dust of the ground, and breathed into nostrils (face) the breath of life and man became a living soul" (Gen. 2:7).

Man is soul because he has the likeness of God and body that links him to earth, and God said, "let us make man in our image, after our likeness" (Gen 1:26-27). He has personality, individuality, intellect-mind, understanding; sensibility-emotions; will-decision.

Man is body because he possesses flesh, bones, nerve, brain, blood—vital organs. "and the Lord God formed man of the dust of the ground" (Gen 2:7). Chemically man has 16 elements of soil represented in his body. Six vital minerals are present in organic form and the remainder being water, carbon and glasses. "the first man is from the earth-earthly..." 1 Cor. 15:47.

By the sweat of your face, shall eat bread, till you return to the ground because from it you were taken, for you are dust." Gen 3:19.

The unregenerate man refers to the natural man. Natural means—the essential quality, essence, or type. Gen. 8:21.

Sin is already present in every human being-rooted-inherited John 3:6. Renewal is a necessity John 3:3, 5; 1:12, 13; Tit. 3:5; Jas. 1:18; 1 Pet 1:3, 23.

Sin blinds and darkness the understanding by destroying the consciousness of divine things. Sin is described in scripture as voluntary ignorance (2 Peter 3:5).

The dark picture of human failure and sorrow is drawn only that the good news the gospel may be more reality received. John 3:16; John 3:18.

Satan and his demons are allowed to be active, but the restraining grace of God keeps demons from all they might wish to do. The Devil, as a successful and roaring lion, prowls about seeking whom he may next devour.

As believers we should respect Satan's cunning and power, but realize that his power is restricted by God (Job 1:12; 2:6; 1 John 4:4). He cannot touch our salvation nor separate us from the love of God (Rom. 8:38-39). We should refuse to be naive, but know that the Bible says about Satan's tactics. Christ has defended our enemies and stripped them of weapons through his death and resurrection (Heb. 2:14-15; Col. 2:15). He prays for us today as he did on earth for the disciples (John 17:15; Luke 22:31-32; 1 John 2:1-2; Heb. 7:25). We have a position of acceptance and authority "in Christ" (Rom 8:1; Eph. 1:6) we have been crucified, raised, and seated with Christ in the heavenlies, far above all demonic authority (Eph. 1:21-22; 2:6). The demons believe and shudder (James 2:19), God may use demonic opposition to cause us to depend more upon him (Job 1-2; 2 Cor. 12:7-10) and God will see us through it all (Rom. 8:28-29).

"Submit yourselves therefore to God. Resist the devil, and he will flee from you." James 4:7. We must confess and renounce all practices and attitudes contrary to God's word (see Exod. 20:4-6). We must put on all the armor of God. Each piece has its purpose and suggests how Satan attacks and how we can resist (Eph. 6:10-18). We must live godly lives for the glory of God. This involves making no provision for sin (Rom. 13:13-14), praying for protection (Matt.

6:13; 26:41), being alert, watching in soberness (1 Thess. 5:6-8; 1 Peter 5:8). We must cultivate our spiritual lives with the word of God (Matt. 4:4), using it against demonic attack (Eph. 6:17). God is ultimately in charge of all things, and we are not to fear (Heb. 13:5; Rom. 8:38-39). He is our refuge and will defeat our enemies (Deut. 33:27; Ps. 27:1-3). Some demons may still be cast out into the abyss, as they were in Jesus' day (Luke 8:32). Ultimately God will punish Satan and all his angels in the lake of fire (Matt. 25:41; Rev. 20:10).

Satan and demons are real, and they are untiringly opposed to God and to his people. Yet,we are more than victors through christ. Let us thank God for perspective given in the scriptures , for the power of Christ and his blood, for protection from the Evil One, and for provision for practical victory in the crucified living savior.

SIX

God's infinite nature is understood through Jesus Christ Involvement

"For this cause came I into the world" (John 18:37) and, again "For the Son of man I come to seek and to save that which was lost" (Luke 19:10). The theme of the sufferings of Christ in death is the ground of all right doctrine and the central facts in this cosmic universe. What did Christ accomplish in his death and sufferings? There are several doctrines that come to our attention.

Substitution means—one taking the place of another (Matt. 20:28; Luke 22:19-20; John 6:51; John 15:13; Rom. 5:6-8; Rom. 8:32; 2 Cor. 5:21; Eph. 5:2; 1 Tim. 2:5-6; Heb. 2:9; 1 Peter 3:18). Vicarious means–one taking the place of another. God cannot look upon sin with the best degree of allowance. As a fallen man stands obligation to God as an offender, he owes an obligation which he could never pay in time or eternity. Unless a vicar shall intervene there is no hope for any member of this fallen race. The Bible teaches without deviation that Christ by His death met the demands of justice on behalf of the sinner. God saves His own people—those who trust Him–from His own wrath (Ps. 38:1; Isa. 60:10; Hos. 6:1; Job. 42:7-8)

In regard to substitution, we have two great features—the gift of eternal life and the gift of righteousness. In John 14:20, we have a relationship. He said "Ye in me, and I in you. Ye in me—our position in Christ (Eph. 1:3). I in you"—eternal life (John 3:36; 1 John 5:11-12). The finished work of Christ has accomplished a trilogy which constitutes benefits to both saved and unsaved. (John 19:30, John 4:34, John 5:36).

Redemption is an sinward aspect of Christ's work on the cross. It is an act of God by which the outraged holiness and government of God requires. It is deliverance from bond servitude. Three words are used to translate redeem.

1. Unsaved are bondsalves in sin (Rom. 7:14; Eph. 2:2; 1 Cor. 12:2). Redeemer must take slaves-place (Matt. 20:28).
2. Unsaved are bond slaves taken out— never again a slave removed.
3. Unsaved are bond slaves set free from sin.

Reconciliation is a manward aspect of Christ's work on the cross. The word reconcile means to change completely. Using those two words in place of reconciliation would represerver its original meaning to change (Rom 11:15; 1 Cor. 7:11; 2 Cor. 5:18; Eph. 2:16). Let us accept God's solution to sin and be satisfied. (Rom. 5:10-11).

Propitiation is the Godward aspect of Christ's work on the cross. (1 John 2:2, 4:10; Rom. 3:25). Christ is the meeting place, the place of communion between a holy God and sinful but believing human beings. Meeting

God in Christ, the believer may boldly say: "who shall lay anything to the charge of God's elect; it is God that justifieth" (Rom. 8:33). God has been rendered free toward sinners by the death of His son for them. Divine responsibility has been perfectly accomplished. By his suffering and death Christ solved the problems of personal sins and the problem of the sin nature. He "died of our sins" (1 Cor. 15:3) and "he died unto sin" (Rom. 6:10). The believer has participated in Christ's crucifixion, death, burial and resurrection (Rom. 6:1-10).

Since this has been accomplished, judgment against the sin nature and the victory over daily sin is possible. To walk after the spirit is to walk in conscious dependence upon the spirit. It is to walk by means of the spirit. (Gal. 5:16).

The spiritual progress of christian may be measured by the growth he makes in "the knowledge of our Lord and Savior Jesus Christ". (2 Pet. 3:18). The believer's conception of Christ who saves him should not only be extended to supernatural proportions but should be increasing with every passing day.

There are three trust set forth by John in his Gospel concerning the Logos: (a) he, as one with God and as God, is from all eternity (1:1-2), (b) He becomes flesh (1:14) and (c) He ever manifests the first person (1:18). To comprehend the relation of the Deity to the world has been the aim of all religious philosophy. The greek word logos signifies that both reason and word. Jesus Christ is the logos of the scripture. He has always been and he ever will be the manifestation of God. The idea is that as a word is the interpreter of the hidden invisible spirit of man, so Jesus, coming forth from the bosom of the father, of Him whom no man hath seen at any time, has revealed Him to us. The world-christ is the living personal manifestation of God to men.

The second scripture is (1 Tim. 3:16)— "And without controversy great is the mystery of godliness; God was manifest in the flesh, justified in spirit, seen of angels, preached unto the Gentiles, believed on in the world, received up into glory".

God was manifest in the flesh.We can comprehend God because of christ. He is a full, clear, impressive-expression of God. His presence among men was the presence of God. (John 5:19; John 6;63; Luke 10:9).

Justified in the spirit. The term logos was applied to Christ by the Holy spirit. It is an identification of who he really is. All that Christ undertook was wrought in perfection which justified it—both in heaven and on earth—being achieved through the eternal spirit. Luke 4:1; Matt. 12:28; Heb. 9:14; John 3:34.

Seen of Angels. From their viewpoint, they have known Him from the time of their creation as their creator and is the object of their ceaseless adoration. They are deeply concerned.

Preached unto the Gentiles. Christ became the way of salvation to every member of the race. Redemption is limitless.

Believed in the world. While Christ was here in the world, a very few sustained this relationship to Him, but they were the beginning of an unnumbered host.

Received up into glory. Christ left this cosmos world and ascended into heaven where his redeeming work was accepted by His father who had sent him into the cosmos world.

"It was God who suffered and it was the blood of God that was shed" Acts 20:28.

Salvation through Christ—Acts 20:28 the word salvation means savior. The word communicates the thought of deliverance, safety, preservation, soundness, restoration and healing. It includes at least 12 extensive and vital doctrines: redemption, reconciliation, propitiation, conviction, repentance, faith, regeneration, forgiveness, justification, sanctification, preservation, and glorification. Salvation provides a dismissal and removal of every charge against the sinner and equips. him with eternal life in place of death, with the perfect merit of Christ in place of condemnation, and with forgiveness and justification in place of wrath.

Salvation includes every divine undertaking for the believer from his deliverance out of the lost estate to his final presentation in glory conformed to the image of Christ (1 Cor. 1:30; Phil. 1:6; Eph. 5:25-27; 1 Thess. 1:9-10; Titus 2:11-13)

The past-tense aspect of our Salvation. At the moment of believing, the saved one is completely delivered from his lost estate, cleansed, forgiven, justified, born of God, clothed in the merit of Christ, freed from all condemnation and safe for evermore. Luke 7:50; Acts 16:30-31; 1 Cor. 3:18; 2 Cor. 2:15; Eph. 2:8.

The present-tense aspect of our salvation. The believer is being saved from the dominion of sin. He is being divinely preserved and sanctified. Rom. 6:1-14; 8:2; 2 Cor. 3:18; Gal. 2:20; 4:19; Phil. 1:19; 2:12; 1 Thess. 2:13.

The future-tense aspect of our salvation. The believer is yet to be saved from the presence of sin when presented faultless in glory. Rom. 13:11; 1 Thess. 5:8; Heb. 1:14; 9:28; 1 Pet. 1:3-5; 1 John 3:1-3.

Through the death of Christ, all judgment and condemnation are so perfectly borne that they can never again be reckoned against the believer—"there is no condemnation to them which are in Christ Jesus" (Rom. 8:1). Our salvation is through Christ.

SEVEN

God's infinite nature is understood through the Church

The Bible says, "Go ye therefore and teach all nations, baptizing them in the name of the father, and of the Son, and of the Holy Ghost: teaching them to observe all things whatsoever I have commanded you: I am with you always, even to the end of the world," (Matt. 28:19, 20). Jesus Christ said earlier, "And I say unto thee, that thou are Peter, and this rock I will build my church; and that gates of hell shall not prevail against it" (Matt. 16:18). The command is clear, concise and comprehensive. Go everywhere and win men to Christ. That is to make Christans, and then baptize them and teach them the truth that I have taught you. The church exists to carry out two foundational functions, evangelism to make disciples and edification to teach them. The church is gathered together in the community to put this purpose into action. The Bible says "but ye shall receive power, after that the Holy Ghost will come upon you, and ye shall be witnesses unto me." (Acts 1:8). Our evangelism ministry is based upon an individual and corporate testimony before the unsaved world, reflecting love, unity and godly living. The Bible says, "wherefore comfort yourselves together, and edify one another, even as also ye do." (1 Thess. 5:11). Our edification ministry involves all the believers in the edification process, ministering to each other. Maturity in the body of Christ is identified with biding faith, hope and love. The program is as follows: the Bible says, "From whom the whole body fitly joined together and compacted by that which every joint supplieth, according to the effectual working in the measure of every part, maketh increase of the body unto the edifying of itself in love." (Eph. 4:16) Every member of the body of Christ is important. Every joint must function and every individual part is to make its contribution to the life of the church. The way to discover your part is to become active in the local church assembly.

The Bible says in Matt. 16:18, "by this rock I will build my church". The church is made up of individuals that believe in the death and resurrection of Christ. they are in Christ, the scripture says in 2 Cor. 5:17-18, "therefore if any man be in Christ, he is a new creature, old things have passed away. Behold all things have become new. And all things are of God who hath reconciled us to Himself by Jesus Christ and hath given us to the ministry of reconciliation." The union which is formed in Christ is deeper than any relationship that the human mind has ever done. The church is the property of Christ to be the sphere of his own infinite person, power and glory.

There are many reasons why we should be in church; because we have a kinship relationship with its member, because the organized church is recognized in the new testament, because it is a duty if the believer, because the church is a self developing body, because we are one in accord in witnessing, because we are to give of our tithes and gifts in obedience, because we are to keep God's memorial supper, and because we love Him who is head of the church, Jesus Christ.

The Bible says, "But an hour is coming and now is, when the true worshipers shall worship the Father in spirit and truth; for such people the father seeks to be His worshipers" (John 4:23). What has happened to true worshipers today? Have we shaped our concepts of God to fit our own understanding? We have measured him by our intellect and felt quite free to expect Him to answer. Have we worshiped only when we decided God has lived up to our expectations? God says, "For as the heavens are higher than earth, so are my ways higher than your ways and My thoughts than your thoughts".(Isa. 55:9)

EIGHT

God's infinite nature is understood through Future Event

Things to come is a study in Biblical Eschatology. It deals with the doctrine of future events.

I have learned to study the Bible from a literal historical grammatical method of interpreting scripture. As a result, I hold to a premillennial, dispensational approach to future things. I further believe in the pre-tribulation rapture of the bride of Christ, a seven year tribulation period followed by the second coming of Christ to set up His literal 1000 years messianic kingdom. After which time satan and all the unrighteous will be judged at the Great White Throne and be cast into the lake of fire forever. The righteous will spend eternity with the Lord in the New Jerusalem. These conclusions come from the book of revelation along with some supportive passages. read about the future and at the same time work for crowns that will be given out,

- Work for incorruptible crown (1 Cor. 9:25).
- Work for a crown of rejoicing (1 Thess 2:19).
- Work for the crown of life
- Work for a crown of righteousness (2 Tim 4:8).

God's Infinite Nature is understood through his perfect plan.

Worship involves three basic activities. The Bible says, "Come, let us worship and bow down" (Ps.95:6). No worship takes place without humbling ourselves. Paul's greatest chapter on humility is Phil. 2, and his greatest chapter on worship is Phil. 3 read them. The one leads to the other. Kneeling goes against the grain of every prideful bone in us but it helps.

Worship involves casting our crowns before the throne (Rev. 4:10). A "Crown" is anything that exalts the wearer. If it draws attention to the person wearing it, then it's a crown. No man who worships. Jesus Christ ever ever wants to be exalted. He is too involved with Christ to demand notice of his own crowns. The third activity of a worshiper of Jesus Chirst is telling the lord His worth-ship. The Bible says, "Worthy art thou, our lord and our God, to receive glory and honor and power" (Rev. 4:11). Get alone often to tell the Lord what He is worth to you. Worship is mandatory. In fact, it's the only essential activity on earth.

God's Infinite Nature is understood through obeying the Holy Spirit

I have learned to live in the positive not in the negative, I have to live with obedience not in disobedience. I have to live with righteousness. I must have divine communion. I must walk as a child of light (Eph. 5:8). These conditions have to be acted upon:

Stop resisting the spirit.
Stop sinning against the spirit.
Stop walking in the flesh

It is simple because we only have to yield our total self to God. It is hard because we have a sinful nature that rebels. We must increase our connection.

"Quench not the spirit" (1 Thess. 5:19). Stop resisting the spirit.we should be in a constant attitude of fellowship not rebellion. We must accept his will and do it. Fellowship and meditation will keep us on the right track.

"Grieve not the spirit (Eph. 4:30). Stop sinful actions. We must practice confession. We must accept forgiveness, we must release evil action from our memory.

Lust not the flesh (Gal. 5:16). Don't be dominated by evil. Let the spirit be in control.

God's Infinite Nature was understood through the Holy Spirit's presences. It takes discipline to practice christianity.

Pray to God for help.

Allow Him to be the priority.

TEN

God's infinite nature is understood through Invitation

The Bible says, "All that the Father giveth me shall come to me."

ROMANS 8:29-30

The invitation is open to you, "Come unto me" (Matthew 11: 28-30). I am grateful for my decision. Have you read Jesus' words, "Come unto me" in Matthew 11:28-30? Have you heard his sweet, deep, sensitive, authentic, bold, eternal, changing words?

"Come unto me" is an open invitation. Let's discover what Jesus means with such awesome words. We will start with a little background.

The Gospel according to Matthew gives a view of the life of Jesus. Most likely, the early accounts were passed on verbally in the Aramaic language and then recorded in Greek manuscripts dating from A.D. 60 to A.D. 90. Matthew emphasizes the Old Testament preparation for the gospel and makes it an ideal "bridge" from the Old and New Testament. Matthew, the Hebrew tax collector, writes for the Hebrew mind. He tells us that Jesus is the Messiah foretold by Old Testament prophets. He starts with the genealogy of Jesus. The coming of Christ to the earth has been anticipated from the beginning. In the early days of human history, God has chosen one family line, that of Abraham, and later on another family in Abraham's line, that of David, to be the family through which His Son would make entrance into the world.

Miracles, lessons learned and many activities have already taken place, but now we have come to Matthew 11:28-30 to think about Jesus' sweet words "come unto me." The purpose of the gospel is to present the good news of the Redeemer-Savior. Jesus is the Messiah of Israel, the Son of God, and the Savior of the world.

The words "come unto me" are life changing words which can't be heard by our sinful, rebellious, and stubborn minds without a sovereignly bestowed spiritual awakening. We have a free offer to all in verses 28-30 and a divine initiative in verse 27. I'm so glad that the Holy Spirit convicts us and that the sovereign work of God is at hand so we can trust our spirit, soul, and body to Jesus Christ. Authority and confidence are found in verse 27. "All things are delivered unto me of my father; and no man knoweth any man the Father, save the Son, and he to whom so ever the Son will reveal him." Jesus is the way initiated by the Father. "My Father" reveals Jesus' absolute equality, He is the "only begotten Son." Personal knowledge of the Father through the Son with the assistance of the Holy Spirit will develop assurance and authority in living. How does genuine conversion take place? The songwriter says, "only trust Him" and the text continues with the answer.

"All ye that labor and are heavy laden" are words that describe our condition. If we are going to hear God's call through Jesus, we have to be in a condition of humility. The labor and burden have brought us to exhaustion and just plain sweat. We have to lay our load at Jesus' feet. Trying to save ourselves will not work. Doing all the good works as well as a guilty conscience will not do it, but a broken heart realizing total dependence is necessary. We will hear His voice, "come unto me" when we recognize our sinful condition. In the present condition we don't measure up to God's standards.

In my childhood, I responded to Jesus. I had been singing with my sisters at a Bible conference. On the way home, our mother asked if we would like to ask Jesus into our hearts. We knew the gospel story. Because of sin, we were separated from God (Romans 3:23), and the penalty for sin is death (Romans 6:23). Thankfully that penalty for sin was paid by Jesus Christ (Romans 5:8). If we repent of the sin — acknowledge need — then confess and trust Jesus as Lord and Savior — accept Jesus — we will be saved (Romans 10:9). Right there in the car on the side of the road, I was "born of God" and a second birth — spiritual — took place (I John 5:11-12). This birth is clearly stated in John 3:8, "The wind bloweth where it listeth, and thou hearest the sound thereof, but cannot tell whence it cometh, and whither it goeth: so is everyone that is born of the Spirit." The wind, which is the same word used for Spirit, cannot be seen or explained. The word can only be heard or observed in relation to its effect. The new birth is spiritual and invisible. One can only observe the results. It's a decision of faith based upon facts. The first element in trusting Jesus is total dependency.

"And I will give you rest . . . ye shall find rest unto your souls" is a powerful claim. It's not only a dependent heart that is necessary but the discovery of divine truth found in Jesus Christ who provides the rest for our souls. Liberation is given through Jesus because of who He is. In the Gospel of John, Jesus is revealed as the eternal, pre-existing Son of God who became man in order to reveal the Father and bring eternal life through His death and resurrection. John says: "Now Jesus did many other signs in the presence of his disciples, which are not written in this book; but these are written that you may believe that Jesus is the Christ, the Son of God, and that believing you may have life in his name" (John 20:30-31).

Jesus is God. "In the beginning was the Word, and the Word was with God, and the Word was God. He was in the beginning with God" (John 1:1). John 1:14 says that "the Word became flesh." The key term, 'Word', refers to Jesus. Jesus is fully God. These phrases are vital to understand. "In the beginning" refers to eternity past. It goes beyond His earthly life, beyond even the beginning of Creation. "With God," refers to an affirmation of Christ's separate personality. There is diversity within the Godhead. "And God was the Word," refers to the fact that Jesus is fully divine in all respects. We can trust Jesus because He is God. He has the authority and power to redeem us and bring us into His family.

"Take my yoke upon you and learn of me; for I am meek and lowly in heart," is a text full of challenges and life changing possibilities. We must turn around in our thinking. We must turn to Jesus and repent. Our way to acceptance and forgiveness are not acceptable. A complete turnaround and a full change of direction is necessary. We have come to the end of our resources. As we learn of Him, we discover our self-regulations. Work-based convictions will not be sufficient. He is gentle and tender and is calling us to Himself. As we turn from our sin and replace it with faith, a new direction takes place. This is not an intellectual exercise but a whole heart change.

"For my yoke is easy and my burden is light," reminds us that salvation in Jesus Christ includes an invitation to surrender. If we want His saving rest, we must take His yoke. The yoke is a symbol of submission. It is used by the master to direct us. Discipline is a natural part of genuine conversion. The yoke is submission to Christ and is not grievous. It is joyous.

My childhood song to live by tells it all, "I have been chosen by the Father, purchased by the Son, and sealed by the Spirit, I'm his very own" (Ephesians 1). As a child, I did not understand everything and even now I still do not. His grace is amazing and His sovereignty is above us. All He wants me to do is take Him at His word. He said, "By one man (Adam), sin entered into the world and death by sin, and so death passed upon all men for all have sinned" (Romans 5:12). "Behold I was shaped in iniquity" (Psalm 51:5). I do not like reading these words, but God said it and I have to accept it. I have discovered that "Ye have chosen me" (John 15:16). "It is God who worketh in you both to will and to do of his good pleasure" (Philippians 2:13). He is drawing me to Himself (John 6:44). He has saved me and called me according to His own purpose and grace (II Timothy 1:9).

I am so glad that I was taught by my parents in the early years that "God commendeth his love toward us in that while we were yet sinners, Christ died for us" (Romans 5:8). As I have grown in Jesus Christ, I have seen His sovereign grace at work. He saved me not by works of righteousness that I have done, but according to His mercy by the working of regeneration and renewing of the Holy Spirit (Titus 3:5).

I live every day knowing "in whom I have believed and am persuaded that he is able to keep that which I have committed unto him against that day" (II Timothy 1:12). Salvation is of the Lord. I am safe because the Father has chosen me, the Son has purchased me and the Holy Spirit has sealed me. Salvation occurs when God changes the heart and unbelievers turn from sin to Christ (Colossians 1:13). Faith is the process for Jesus to enter the heart and dwell there (Ephesians 3:17). Praise the Lord! As I learn to follow Jesus, life will become a celebration because it involves His supernatural power.

God's infinite nature is understood through Security

The Bible says, "I have written unto you that believe . . . that ye may know."

JOHN 1:12-13

Learning to live every moment in God's presence requires a personal relationship. My confidence is secure because I am assured of my relationship with Christ.

- Salvation is assured through God's Word (I John 5:11, 12).

  "And this is the record, that God hath given to us eternal life and this life is in his Son. He that hath the Son hath life and he that hath not the

Son of God hath not life. These things have I written unto you that believe on the name of the Son of God; that ye may know . . ."

- Salvation is assured through God's authority (John 1:12, 13).

  "But as many as received him, to them gave he power to become the Sons of God, even to them that believe on his name; which were born, not of blood, nor of the will of the flesh, nor of the will of man, but of God."

- Salvation is assured through God's security (John 10:27-30).

  "My sheep hear my voice and I know them, and they follow me: And I give unto them eternal life, and they shall never perish, neither shall any man pluck them out of my hand. My Father, which gave them to me, is greater than all, and no man is able to pluck them out of my Father's hand — I and my Father are one."

- Salvation is assured through God's grace (Ephesians 2:8-9).

"For by grace are ye saved through faith, and that not of yourselves; it is the gift of God, not of works, lest any man should boast."

- Salvation is assured through God's justice (I Peter 3:18).

  "For Christ also hath once suffered for sins, the just for the unjust, that he might bring us to God, being put to death in the flesh but quickened by the Spirit."

- Salvation is assured through God's love (Romans 5:8).

  "But God commendeth his love toward us, in that while we were yet sinners, Christ died for us."

- Salvation is assured through God's transformation (II Corinthians 5:17).

  "Therefore if any man be in Christ, he is a new creature: old things are passed away and behold all things are become new."

God's presence involves a relationship that is secure.

TWELVE

God's infinite nature is understood through Perspective

The Bible says, "The spirit giveth life."

II CORINTHIANS 3:6

Sometimes life is cruel and full of suffering, physically and psychologically. Sometimes our expectations for life fail, there is little meaning to life, there is desperation and despair, or there is just a falling out in the realities of life. The Word carries with it no uncertainties. I can be sure of the faithfulness of God in fulfilling His promises. With hope, I have conviction and assurance. I want to become contagious with encouragement and endurance that springs from hope.

Those with difficult and long-standing problems or are misled in regard to their problems need hope. Those who are harassed by fear, have dashed hopes, or have failed often need hope. People who have experienced dramatic life changes, fallen into depression, or suffered life-shattering experience need hope.

When I find myself searching for help, I find it in the hope that I have in Jesus. I have learned through Psalm 39:1-13 that my innermost thoughts toward the wicked should be confident and not complaining. I should be watchful of what I say (v.1-2). My innermost thoughts toward God should be honest and not with a bitter attitude. I must share my anguish and pain with God (v.3-4). When I am searching for hope, my innermost thoughts toward myself should not be deceiving. I have to learn God's perspective on life (v.5-6). *My innermost thoughts toward deliverance should be Scripture-directed (v.7-13).* I have learned that in despair, I can experience confidence (v.7), in confession I can be released (v.8), and that correction is needed sometimes (v.9-11). I have been comforted (v.12-13).

I am discovering with excitement that in Jesus Christ's name, I can live with hope and obtain the help I need. He is worth believing. There is no one whose understanding of life has come close to His. Jesus is in the life changing business. All kinds of people have come to Him: the messed-up, sick, injured, forgotten, and despised. Even the satisfied, admired, worthy and religious people. I have come to Him. Jesus has been changing lives for two thousand years. I am learning to leap out of my comfort zone into faith. I realized that there must be less of me and more of Him. Not only do I have to let go of myself and replace myself with Him, I also have to learn to wait. This is the in-between period. When I hold onto His promise, "My hope is in Jesus . . . hear my prayer, O Lord, listen to my cry for help" (Psalm 39:7,12). I know victory will come because He keeps to His word. Some adjustments have to be made during the waiting time until victory. As I apply the attributes of

God to the names given to Jesus, I will be given God's perspective.

His name is Wonderful (Isaiah 9:6). I believe in an awesome God. He can make my life wonderful because He is wonderful. My first adjustment in obtaining help is believing that He is awesome. Wonderful things have happened, are happening, and will continue to happen. It all starts with experiencing forgiveness of sin and the invasion of a whole new life. "Christ liveth in me" (Galatians 2:20). Believing in Jesus is required (Acts 16:31). He wants intimate fellowship. "I count all things to be a loss in view of the surpassing value of knowing Christ Jesus my Lord" (Philippians 3:7-8). Knowing God is the most important thing I can accomplish. My goal is to know Him so well that I can confidently say, "I have received a spirit of adoption as sons by which I cry, 'Abba! Father!'" The word 'Abba' is equivalent to 'Daddy'. It is a term of respect and endearment.

As a continuation of this first adjustment, I can better understand how I am to live by truly knowing God. As I contemplate God's attributes through His names, I have been promised strength, encouragement, and help. I know God loves me. God is love and the one who abides in love abides in God and God abides in Him (I John 4:16). I am surrounded with His infinite person, power, and glory (John 14:20). "And I will pray the Father, and He shall give you another Comforter, that He may abide with you forever . . . I am in my Father, and ye in me, and I in you" (v.16, 20). He says, "I am in you." He is more than me, He is *in* me. He also supplies in Himself all that any soul will ever need in time or for eternity. The union I have 'in Christ' is beyond my comprehension. The oneness that I have with Jesus means many things (John 17:20-23). My emphasis here is fellowship. It is awesome to say that I have an everlasting companionship with Him. In the place we live, He abides. I am looking for the eternal security which starts here and now as I draw near to Him. "To be in Christ" refers to my position with or my union to Christ. In believing, I have that relationship and possession of the divine. I am safe in His hands because I am associated with the Creator-Redeemer God. *"Christ in me" refers to transformation power.*

His name is Counselor. I believe in an all-knowing God. He is my counselor. He knows everything. "Who has directed the Spirit of the Lord or as His counselor has informed Him? With whom did He consult and gave Him understanding? And who taught Him in the path of justice and taught Him knowledge, and informed Him of the way of understanding?" (Isaiah 40:13-14). God knows what He knows simply because He knows it. He did not learn it. The second adjustment is to accept His counsel. He is qualified to counsel me. He is eternal God in whom "dwelleth all the fullness of the Godhead bodily" (Colossians 2:9). Jesus Christ was a part of the eternal counsel of creation. He was there when the Father said, "Let us make man." He understands me because He became man. He is able to enter into the experiences that perplex and burden me. He knows my heart and mind. He is able to help me understand myself. I have to let go of myself and let Him take over.

I must learn to sit back and watch Him work. He knows my feelings, desires, personality, and disease. He has known everything from the beginning (Acts 15:18). Nothing can escape His all-encompassing knowledge. I have learned that God permits trials for reasons we may or may not understand, but He is able to bring good out of the worst circumstances. I am able to have confidence because He knows all the possibilities. He is personal. The Bible says, "O Lord, thou hast searched me and known me" (Psalm 139:1-2). He knows my thought process (Ezekiel 11:5). God is concerned about the details; He knows everything going on behind the scenes (Job 23:10).

His name is Mighty God. I believe in a powerful God. Jesus is God Himself. There is nothing God cannot do. His unlimited power will reflect His divine glory and accomplish His sovereign will. "Power belongs to God" (Psalm 62:11). He is able to "call into being that which does not exist" (Romans 4:17). "He spoke and it was done" (Psalm 33:6). "Nothing is impossible with God" (Luke 1:37). The Scripture says, "Thou hast formed my inward parts . . . I am fearfully and wonderfully made" (Psalm 139:13-14). God's power is very personal. "Thy will be done" (Matthew 5) is my prayer. He is able to deliver (Daniel 3:17). He is able to keep me standing in His presence (Jude 24). He says to "be strong in the Lord and in the strength of His might" (Ephesians 6:10). The third adjustment for change is embracing the fact that He is "Mighty God." He is called "Immanuel" which means 'God with us.' I have to understand His claims and accept His deity. With that response, I am strengthened with all might. He takes care of the demands of life. No matter what the problem, He has the power to meet it, handle it, solve it, and use it for my good and for His glory.

His name is Everlasting Father. I believe in a sovereign God. He is the originator of eternity. I live in a new dimension of life. God has absolute rule and control over all His creation. God rules absolutely over the affairs of men. God can do whatever He wants simply because it is all His.

"The earth is the Lord's and all it contains, the world, and those who dwell in it" (Psalm 24:1). Everything that occurs does so under the hand of a sovereign God. The fourth adjustment for change is reveling in His name, the everlasting Father. God has created me for eternity and Jesus Christ came to earth to reveal eternity (I John 1:1, 2). There is more to life than what my senses reveal. In trusting Jesus, I am able to meet every detail of life with confidence. I am safe in Jesus because of who He is. I exist for Him. I can live in confidence because Jesus provides strength. There are no chance happenings. Whatever happens, it will bring good (Psalm 8:28). He has the whole picture. I can trust in Jesus and He is able to guard what I have entrusted to Him (2 Timothy 1:12).

His name is Prince of Peace. I believe in an intimate God. The fifth adjustment for change is peace. When I accomplish the alignment process through His grace, I will experience peace. Do not try to change the circumstances but change in character. In reality, peace does not come from the outside in, but from the inside out. I am learning that my testing, trials, and temptations can become a win-win situation. I must learn to let go of self. I must learn to make the adjustments. I must learn to practice victory in peace. He is free from the limitations of space. He is everywhere present. He is in me (I John 4:4). I believe in an awesome God because He is wonderful in all His acts. He wants fellowship with me. I believe in an all-knowing God because He provides wise counsel. He has all knowledge. He knows my inner needs. I believe in a powerful God because there is nothing He cannot do. He is in control. When I reflect upon these facts and allow them to penetrate my spirit, soul, and body, I am able to face today.

As I repeat the names of Jesus with a sincere heart and allow the Holy Spirit to enable me, I will be encouraged. This is a starting point. Authentic transformation takes time because it is a process. It is not a formula to follow; it is not a list of basic principles to apply. It is not a mechanical determination. It is faith working in me through the Holy Spirit's guidance and power. "May the God of hope fill you with all joy and peace as you trust in him, so that you may overflow with hope by the power of the Holy Spirit" (Romans 15:13).

The promise of help is provided through Jesus. I am thankful for the Lord's presence. This chapter was written when I started a new journey in my life. I am facing a fearful, dreadful uncertainty in my health. The biopsy has returned with a positive result. Cancer is the disease. I was told that my cancer is the second top killer of man. That information was really discouraging. I am waiting for the details and what treatment options I have. I do not like the side effects of any of them. I still need to know the facts. The initial shock has worn off. My family is very supportive. I know their prayers and spiritual perspective will continue to be helpful.

My daughter shared a prayer and Psalm 91:11, which says, "He who dwells in the shelter of the Most High will rest in the shadow of the Almighty." She has started a network of prayer support. My son immediately gave me a verse from Hosea 6:3, "Let us acknowledge the Lord . . . as surely as the sun rises He will appear . . . He will come to us." He has also set up a network of prayer warriors. I am so pleased that they have accepted this challenge in the way that they have. They know what works and what pleases God. Without them knowing it, both Bible references reinforce the verse the Holy Spirit gave to me and my wife, James 4:8, "Draw near to God and He will draw near to you." My dark thoughts have turned to the light because Jesus is wonderful. My folly has turned to wise thinking because Jesus is my counselor. Losing heart has changed to a conquering spirit because Jesus is my mighty God. I have been drawing closer to my everlasting Father who holds eternity in His hands. When I think of these names of Jesus, peace from the Prince of Peace has entered my spirit. "Jesus is the sweetest name I know and He's just the same as His lovely name, and that's the reason why I love Him so, O Jesus is the sweetest name I know."

THIRTEEN

God's infinite nature is understood through Miracles

The Bible says, ". . . the beginning of miracles and the disciples believed."

JOHN 2:4

Supernatural events of Jesus Christ give evidence that belief and faith count. Memorize John 2:11. "This beginning of miracles did Jesus in Cana of Galilee and manifested his glory and his disciples believed on him." God exists in Jesus Christ. Miracles are a part of the historical evidence. Read the first gospels with an open heart and the Holy Spirit will give you understanding.

Meditate on the supernatural activity of Jesus Christ. They will produce motivation that belief and faith work. The miracles represent relationship building, personal need, supernatural touch, and conviction to follow Christ. Let's look at each miracle and ponder over it. Look at your personal life and see if miracles are happening today.

Turn Water into Wine (John 2:1-11)
A small-town pastor receives a gracious gift: a cow and freezer from a farmer in town. It was a necessary need.

Orders the Wind and the Waves (Mark 4:35-41)
A music minister was forced to leave church and drive home through a tornado storm. The car shook; it was dangerous, but Christ calmed the wind.

Walk on Water (Matt 19:22-33)
A young pastor was called to a teenager suicide event. She was hanging from a tree. The family needed comfort and understanding. Christ brought peace in the bad situation.

Raises Lazarus to Life (John 11:17-44)

A musician/minister/mentor would stay alive on a heart machine. He suffered two heart attacks and congestive heart failure and now open-heart surgery. Jesus Christ was the strength for family and him.

Cure a Man of Evil Spirit (Mark 5:1-20)

An associate pastor called to help a man who was a Satan worshiper. He learned about Jesus Christ and was delivered. It is a remarkable story.

Heals Crippled Man (Mark 2:1-12)

A pastor's heart was weakened through the death of his wife. A terrible accident took place but in the situation, he glorified God and was blessed.

FOURTEEN

God's infinite nature is understood through Passion

The Bible says, "My heart says seek him."

PSALM 27:4, 5

One thing I ask of the Lord that I may dwell in the house of the Lord all the days of my life, to gaze upon the beauty of the Lord and to seek Him in His temple, For in the day of trouble, He will keep me safe . . . my heart says of you, seek His face! Your face Lord, I will seek" (Psalm 27:4, 5, 8). This means with intensity. In the previous verse, a strong affirmation has been recorded. "The Lord is my light and my salvation, whom shall I fear" (v.1-3). The New Testament counterpart to this is, "If God be for us, who can be against us" (Romans 8:31). My life is and will continue to be wrapped with His arms (v.4-5). I will have a sense of His protection and will not worry but music will flow into my heart (v.6).

Some people think that Jesus was just God. Others think that He was just a man, or just an angel. Some think that He was an angel and a man. ***I believe that Jesus was and is God incarnate, which means that He is both God and man.*** Jesus was born of a human mother (Galatians 4:4). He grew up like any other human being (Luke 2:52). He was hungry (Matthew 4:4) and thirsty (John 19:28). He grew weary and needed rest (John 4:6). He felt sadness and cried (John 11:35). He suffered (John 19:1), died (John 19:33) and was buried (John 19:40-42). He was human in every sense that we are, yet He was without sin (Hebrews 4:15).

I have discovered that He is one person who has two natures, human and divine. Jesus, God the Son, existing as the second person of the triune God, united His divine nature to a human nature, and came into the world through that. He did not stop being God when He added humanity to Himself. Remember, God has no limitations. We are "one-dimensional beings", and He is not. In Deuteronomy 6:4, it says "Yahweh, our God; Yahweh is a plurality within an indivisible unity." God is one divine nature shared by three persons — the Father, Son, and Holy Spirit. God the Son has an infinite nature assumed in addition to a finite nature. There is one divine nature, or essence, of God. In Jesus Christ, we have added a human nature. Jesus is the Son of God (Lord) and Son of Man (Savior).

I am convinced that Jesus Christ can do whatever He wills to do according to His character. Jesus is my spiritual and physical healer. Whatever my needs are, He already knows about them. He knows how I will react or act toward them. He knows what works for me and what is best for me. My decision is simply, "Thy will be done." I have a growing passion for Jesus Christ. In my intense search, He will make me free in my need. He said, "If you remain in my word, you are truly my disciples and you will know the truth and the truth will make you free" (John 8:31, 32).

I have confidence in Him because of who He is. If I learn to do what He says to do, I will have continual assurance of His presence, power, and peace. These characteristics will be flowing through my veins because I learned to take His perspective in all things. Real hope for me is freedom and growth found in God's grace. Everything I have been writing about seems to be a mystery. It works if I gaze upon Jesus and obey His Word. The Scripture starts with "If you . . ." I must respond with my head and heart to the gospel. In my childhood, I received Jesus into my life and began a growing relationship. The Christian walk is hard and can be a struggle because the old nature is fighting against it. I have and will continue to relinquish my will to Jesus because true liberation comes when my heart says "yes" to God's words "follow me."

In my billfold, I carry a pastoral prescription card. It refreshes my mind to do certain things if

I want freedom. Many things can go wrong and bring pain, confusion, worry, and struggle. My health, finances, addictions, motives, decisions, self-esteem, confidence, etc. can easily be affected. *As I continually gaze upon Jesus, I will be set free.* The prescription offers a Biblical solution. It is an "exchange strategy" (Philippians 4:6-9). I am learning to recite appropriate Scripture to meet my needs. His perspectives, with prayer and thanksgiving, replace mine. Reflection follows with His presence providing reason for praise and positive memories. This will lead to reliance on His promises which becomes habitual meditation. Thinking right becomes an ordinary practice. His perspective, presence, promises, and power take over in my life pattern and bring peace and a single focus. Jesus is indeed my passion.

FIFTEEN

God's infinite nature is understood through Justification

The Bible says, "Jesus was delivered for our justification and was raised for our justification."

ROMANS 4:25

herefore as by the offense of one judgment came upon all men to condemnation; even so by the righteousness of one the free gift came upon all men unto justification of life" (Romans 5:18). Justification means to acquit or to declare righteous. It is a legal term used for a favorable verdict in a trial. No one can withstand God's judgment (Romans 3:9-20). The law was not given to justify sinners but to expose their sin. To remedy our lost, condemned situation, God sent His Son to die for our sins in our place. When we believe in Jesus, God imputes His righteousness to us. God is both a righteous judge and the one who declares us righteous. He is our justifier (Romans 3:26).

I am justified through Christ's death. Scientific historical evidence proves that the crucifixion took place. Justification starts with a relationship with Jesus Christ. Redemption takes place when we acknowledge what God has done. Believe in your heart the truth. Salvation comes through acknowledgement, belief, and confession. Justification is through faith alone (1:16, 17; 3:24). I was standing with love and confidence in court. The judge thought I was a representative and substitute. The addicted teenager needed help, not jail. I was willing to help as a representative of the boy. I represented the church. The judge thought I was a lawyer, but I told him I was the boy's pastor, and seeking the best possible means for him. The judge wanted to meet with me after the trial. He took his robe off and shook my hand. He said he appreciated what I did for the boy and that he had many more boys and girls who needed representatives like me. He asked if I wanted to help them. This was the beginning of a new ministry for me.

SIXTEEN

God's infinite nature is understood through Resurrection

The Bible says, "These are many infallible proofs."

ACTS 1:3

The God of the Bible is the true God. Christ was not made but declared the Son of God by the resurrection (Romans 1:4). Jesus Christ bases His authority of claims and teachings on His resurrection (John 2:13-22). The resurrection of Jesus Christ alone gives certainty. The resurrection is God's seal on Christ's claim to divinity.

There are "many infallible proofs" of the resurrection (Acts 1:3). The book of Matthew says that it was "very early on the first day of the week" (28:1). The book of Mark says, "It was very early on the first day of the week" (16:2). The book of Luke says that it was "at early dawn" (24:1). The book of John says, "it was still dark" (20:1). Read about these people — Matthew, Mary Magdalene, Mark, Mary the mother of James, Luke, Joanna, John, and Peter.

The sightings of Jesus on His resurrection give a solid answer to the question given to me, "Why do I believe in Jesus Christ?" Jesus Christ is my "Mighty God and Counselor" (Isaiah 9:6). He has directed me, using His people, circumstances, and decisions to guide in my life. Even in the small details, His sovereignty is experienced. My main goal in my life and studies is to know Jesus Christ. He is the foundation of all sound knowledge and learning.

SEVENTEEN

God's infinite nature is understood through Cleansing

The Bible says, "Be reconciled to God and become righteous."

II CORINTHIANS 5:20, 21

Supernatural cleansing is the new birth. Wrap yourself around Christ. I am obtaining knowledge of God. The word 'know' is knowledge. It's not only intellectual understanding of truth but *a living participation* in the truth (I John 17:3). "This is life eternal, that they might *know* thee the only true God, and Jesus Christ . . ." I belong to Christ. I am in union with Him, I am united to Him. I am in His family. Cleansing is the process in trusting a person. Jesus Christ is the Savior (I Peter 1:11; 2:12; 3:2; 5:18). God and Savior are not two different people. Christ is God and Savior (II Peter 1:1). In order to be our Savior, He had to give His life on the cross and die for the sins of the world. When we trust Jesus Christ as our Savior, His righteousness becomes our righteousness, and we are given a right standing before God. Supernatural cleansing takes place (II Corinthians 5:21). It is a gift of God to those that believe. Grace is God's favor to the undeserving. God channels grace to us through Jesus Christ (John 1:16). God's righteousness and grace provides the experience of peace (Romans 5:11; Philippians 4:6-7). Supernatural cleansing is introduced through knowledge of the truth.

I understand that cleansing finds its authority in Jesus Christ. A response to church, service, experience, and doctrine are essential for spiritual growth, yet understanding Christ transcends them all. I have to understand who Christ is and be identified with Him in His redemptive work (John 8:12, 32). He is my source of values, our authority, and our goals. Notice these facts about Christ. They convince me and provide conviction and confidence.

- Christ was involved in the creation of the world (Col.1:16).
- Christ was totally God (I John 1:1-3).
- Christ decided to be born (Matthew 1:16).
- Christ became human without sin (I John 1:6-18).
- Christ became the spotless Lamb of God.

Supernatural cleansing has its authority in Jesus Christ.

Man is body because he possesses flesh, bones, nerves, brain, blood, and vital organs. "And the Lord God formed man of the dust of the ground (I Corinthians 15:47). Notice these facts about man and his condition:

- Man was created by God (Genesis 1:1).
- Man was created in God's image (Genesis 1:26).

- Man was born in sin (Ephesians 2:8).
- Man is dependent on God (I John 5:28).
- Man is a soul (Genesis 1:26-27).
- Man is a body (Genesis 2:7).

I believe man is a spirit because he is dependent upon God. The breath of God was an endless life not subject to death. ". . . may your spirit and body be preserved complete, without blame at the coming of our Lord Jesus Christ (I Thessalonians 5:23). God's image refers to spirit, soul, and body. "Let us make man in our image" (Genesis 1:26-27). Supernatural cleansing involves spiritual transformation.

I believe in the divine plan of God, when before the foundations of the world, He unconditionally chose those whom He would save (Romans 8:28-30; John 6:44). God's foreknowledge is more than part of His omniscience. It is a relationship established with the elect before the world began (II Timothy 2:19; I Peter 1:20). Notice these facts about salvation:

- God unconditionally chose souls to be saved (Romans 8:28-30).
- God has become a substitute (II Corinthians 5:21).
- God has provided redemption (I Peter 1:21).
- God is my reconciliation (I John 2:2).
- God prepared the way (John 10:28-30).
- God prepared a Christ-centered life (John 16:2-4).

The new birth produces an inner spiritual cleansing.

"Not by works of righteousness which we have done, but according to his mercy He saved us, by the **washing of regeneration** and **renewing of the Holy Ghost,**" (Titus 3:5). The new birth produces a living hope.

"Blessed be the God and Father of our Lord Jesus Christ, which according to his abundant mercy hath **begotten us unto a living hope,** by the resurrection of Jesus Christ from the dead," (I Peter 1:3). The new birth produces a life characterized by righteousness.

"If ye know that he is righteous ye know that **every one that doeth righteousness is born of him,**" (I John 2:29). The new birth produces a life characterized by freedom.

"**Whosoever is born of God doth not commit [practice] sin,** for his seed remaineth in him, and he cannot [practice] sin, because he is born of God," (I John 3:9). The new birth produces a life characterized by love.

"We know that we have passed from death unto life, because we love the brethren. He that loveth not his brother abideth in death…Beloved, let us love one another, for love is of God and **every one that loveth is born of God and knoweth God,**" (I John 3:14; 4:7). The new birth produces a life characterized by obedience.

"For this is the love of God, that we keep his commandments, and his commandments are not grievous. **For whatsoever is born of God overcometh the world** and this is the victory that overcometh the world, even our faith," (I John 5:3-4). The new birth enables one to know and believe the truth.

"**Whosoever believeth that Jesus is the Christ is born of God**, and every one that loveth him that begat loveth him also that is begotten of him," (I John 5:1). Supernatural cleansing is secure in our believing.

EIGHTEEN

God's infinite nature is understood through Action

The Bible says, "I am a doer of the word."

JAMES 1:22

Faith is a response of trust in a person, based upon that individual's character and word, which issues in action.

My Responsibility

I will move forward as I practice faith. God's plan will work as I become responsible. My responsibility is to respond to God on the basis of what is said in the Scripture. I cannot earn the grace of God. I must "hear faith" (Galatians 3:2-3).

My belief is not based on rules and forms but believing and receiving the baptism of the Spirit by the "hearing of faith."

My Action

Faith is much more than an intellectual assent to a group of ideas. It is an action. The Bible says, "Remembering without ceasing your work of faith, and labor of love and patience of hope in our Lord Jesus Christ, in the sight of God and our Father" (I Thessalonians 1:3). Genuine faith is a practice. It deals with the way I live. Every day, I must make a decision to accept God's will and glorify Him. I will overcome as I love, be patient, and hope in Jesus Christ.

My Strength

My strength is nourished on the words of faith. These words refer to the basis of my faith in the Scriptures. The word of God is the very foundation for what we are to believe as well as the blueprint. In my troubled time facing ill health from head to toe, the Scripture has become my resource. Strength is provided (I Timothy 4:6). I will and have attained it. I am thankful for the Bible. It has truly been my source of strength.

My Warfare

I have been reminded that I have a fight on my hands. Since I belong to the Lord Jesus Christ, a war is going on. The devil hates the Savior and can only strike out at Him and His people. I also have a conflict with the world as well as my fleshly desires. I have to choose to praise the Word of God. I will receive divine protection (I Timothy 6:12). The Bible is powerful. It's a big exercise to see it in action. Through faith I am using His promise to obtain victory.

My Certainty

Doubt and fear will come into my presence. I have to learn that there is a union of the Scriptures and faith. There comes to pass a spiritual act whereby the promises of God and my faith are united and become one. Faith is the body of truth believed (II Timothy 4:7). Faith is the response of submission, obedience, and trust (John 1:12). There is a response of faith and the word of God united. My certainty is assured. I cannot separate the true act of believing from that which is believed.

My Relationship

Let's keep in memory that Jesus is the author and finisher of our faith (Hebrews 12:2). He has given me the gift of faith. He will sustain me. He makes it possible to enter into His presence in heaven. I live with trials, confusion, frustration, and disappointment. But with a serious attempt, I can choose genuine faith.

My Possession

I am a doer of His word (James 1:22). I possess God's precious faith (II Peter 1:1). The word 'precious' shows me the value of faith. The highest value in life is spiritual. The most priceless benefits are found in grace. I want to be characterized with faith, love, and hope. Obedience, fruitfulness, joy, and peace are included. Faith is Jesus' plan for me to succeed. Each thought will draw me closer to Him.

My Sin

The Bible tells us that all people are sinful. That's probably not what you wanted to hear! In our culture, the word sin is not often used. People don't like to think of themselves as sinful or label others as sinful. But in reality, sin is a disease that infects the entire human race. No group of people is exempt from sin. At the heart of all the troubles in the world lies sin. Where does this sin come from? If we examine the first book of the Bible we see right away that sin entered God's perfect world of creation through the deception of Satan (see Genesis 3). Satan is the enemy of God and therefore the enemy of all humans.

My Choice

The gospel is the "Good News," the news that Christ died for us and rose again for our sins. Why is the news so good? Well, the Good News makes a new person out of you. You cannot change on your own. You cannot enter heaven on your own. You cannot live a full and complete life on your own. If you respond with your mind and heart to the gospel, you will see a change in your life. I have studied different religions, human nature, and my own behavior, which has led me to realize that the gospel is the only answer to the challenges of human existence. Jesus Christ is the only way.

We have learned the facts concerning our sin, and it demands a personal response. I had to make a decision to believe what God had to say and to trust Jesus Christ as my only hope for forgiveness and eternal life (John 10:9; Acts 20:21). It has been the most important decision of my life. Have you made that choice? If not, just pray:

"Dear God, I know that I am a sinner. I believe that You sent Your Son to die on the cross to pay the penalty for my sin. I put my faith in You and trust You completely. Come into my heart and control my life. Thank You Lord."

If you prayed that prayer, you can be assured that you are now a Christian. Contact me, and I will help you grow in your new life!

NINETEEN

God's infinite nature is understood through Faith

The Bible says, ". . . look unto Jesus the author and finisher of our faith."

HEBREWS 12:1, 2

"Let us draw near to him." The troubled heart in part will vanish when I answer the question, "How do I draw near to Jesus to prepare for heaven?" It is through accepting the exercise of faith in Jesus. I like reading God's Word. Sometimes I only read a verse or two at a time. I listen to the impression it makes upon my spirit. My soul reacts with delight and talks to God through prayer. Faith requires thinking and illumination from the Holy Spirit. I need to know the meaning of faith and how to live victoriously with it. It starts with God speaking, "let us run with patience the race that is set before us. Looking unto Jesus the author and finisher of our faith" (Hebrews 12:1, 2). The theme of Hebrews is a solemn warning against the coming short of victory and encouragement to press on in spite of all my difficulties. Faith is the challenge. I remember in my childhood I learned a broad meaning of the word faith — "forsaking all I trust him." I want to build on its meaning. Remember that willful sinning, deliberate, and continued disobedience and failure to judge known sin may result in "falling away." This results in God's judgement with only one purpose in mind – that of correction, not damnation.

I can have victory through faith. Victory implies a battle. Salvation is free, but victory means sacrifice. To win the race requires discipline. To experience victory, I have to understand faith. Conquering faith is what I am interested in. My childhood faith was easy. I took God at His

Word. In the uncertainties of my adult life, I have to do the same thing. I believe the unreasonable, impossible, and inexplainable because Someone else in whom I have absolute confidence has said it was so. Upon His Word, I believe it without asking any further proof (Hebrews 11:1-3).

I accept the truth simply upon the word of someone else and without proof or any other evidence. It is believing what I cannot see, hear, feel taste, smell, or understand. It is confidence in another. Who do I trust? My belief in God is based upon the record of His Word. This is backed up by an eternity of faithfulness. No one who has ever put his trust in Him has ever been lost or disappointed (I John 5:9, 10). I think it all goes back to Genesis 1:1. The natural man wants to reason out the origin of the universe and come up with a thousand speculations. The believer rests upon the simple statement of God: "In the beginning, God created the heavens and the earth." God does not stop to explain. He is not obliged to satisfy my curiosity or stoop to satisfy my mental concerns. He is absolute, final, and true. This first verse of the Bible is the first example of faith. If I can believe that He spoke everything into existence and that He has no beginning or end, I can believe anything else He has to say. I can believe all the miracles: that He could become man and be God, that He prepared for my redemption, that His blood can cleanse me, and that He is the author of faith and its authority.

The victory of faith is won through sacrifice. It is a battle and will cause wounds, scars, and disappointments, yet in the end will be a glorious crown of victory. He requires me to surrender for service, to separate myself from the world, to abstain from sinful pleasures, and to refuse to compromise with evil (Romans 12:2).

I absolutely need to know how to grow in faith since it is the key to living eternally. How do I live victoriously on a daily basis on my route to heaven? I have learned that worship starts the faith process. I must start with the Lamb of God. The foundation is in my salvation in Jesus Christ. He is the giver of faith. He provides the direction, guidance, authority, and confidence. Religious activities are not the means. It is through my daily devotion to Him (John 4:23) and relationship development. My worship will take me from the present to eternity, and from eternity to unending life with Christ. It will become a Holy Spirit-stimulated vitality. True worship requires me to approach God with my whole person. It is a love for God in gratitude for what He has done. I have to experience an intimate relationship with God. My invisible part, or spirit, must meet with God. My entire being is activated through love (Matthew 22:37, 38). To understand faith requires God-consciousness through praying, praising, reading the Bible, thoughtful meditations, etc. Faith will grow when I make the choice to be sensitive to God's will. I have to practice the presence of God. My union with Jesus Christ will establish a reliant trust and reverent worship.

The faith process starts with worship and will continue with a walk that glorifies Jesus Christ. I have to ask myself the question, "how deep is my fellowship with Jesus?" Developing communion with Jesus Christ begins by recognizing His residence in me. At the same time, my faith will grow because the foundation is sound. The divine genius of the Scriptures, the Holy Spirit, is my indwelling helper and counselor. A change has taken place because I have made a confession of faith (Romans 10:9, 10). With that confession, the Holy Spirit dwells in me (Romans 8:9). I have a tremendous responsibility: will Christ be magnified in my body? The top priority is always to die to self. Yielding to God's will and dedication to Jesus as Lord is necessary. His indwelling presence is not in my imagination, but the real thing.

The divine transformation will take place when I answer the question, what does it mean to be Christ-centered? Jesus says give me your body and mind. I have to learn to respond to Jesus' demands. He is the dominate influence in my life. Applied Christianity is spiritual transformation. This involves sound doctrine, renewing of the mind, behavioral change, and a willing heart.

The divine transformation will lead to the divine will. God will work His will in me. He is shaping me into the image of His Son. Each day belongs to Him, and I must surrender all to Him. His will is that I understand that the mind controls the body, the will controls the mind, and the Spirit leads the way. I have to learn to just let go of self and let God do it. He will accomplish His will (Romans 12:1, 2).

The faith process involves sincere worship, a surrendered walk, and sacrificial work. My work ethic is based upon eternity. "Work for the night is coming" (John 9:4). This phrase has led the way to many projects. Faith has opened the door. When worship has the proper motivation, it will prepare me to have the correct mindset – biblical spirituality. When my walk, or behavior, is Christ-centered, it will prepare me to live out what I believe within. The faith process will be reflected in the work God has given me to do. The proclamation of the Word through music, ministry, and mentoring all have been built upon each other. It has been a joyful experience to reflect on His work being accomplished. Victorious faith will continue with a restful spirit in my life as I worship with sincerity, as I walk in surrender, and as I work sacrificially. The Old Testament heroes of faith like Abel, Enoch, and Noah will be my examples. "I will run the race with patience . . . looking upon Jesus the author and finisher of my faith" (Hebrews 2:1-3).

Epilogue

I am compelled to answer these questions after writing Discovering God's Infinite Nature. I have strength for His character and compassion. I kneel in awe at God's splendor and majesty.

1. Who made God?
2. How can you be sure that there is a God?
3. How do you define God?
4. How do I talk to God?
5. Why has God placed me on earth?

1. Who made God

The Bible says in Gen. 1:1, "In the beginning, God created heaven and the earth." in the beginning in the Hebrew means literally "in the head of all things". It is a term which refers to the absolute beginning before which there is nothing but eternity. It was the beginning of the universe and we know it. Behind this beginning , there was nothing which is now part of the material world. As far as what may be said about what lies in the vast timeless eternity before creation, man is very limited. From the beginning, God knows the end, and from the end he knows the beginning. To really understand this, you need to understand the intellect of God. God is defined by His attributes to declare His person and the sum total of His attributes, would constitute a final definition of God. God is a personality. He has intellect, sensibility, and will. He comprehends all things, things past, things present, and things future. Man's position before God is standing in awe.

God is able to do whatever He wills, but He may not will to do the full measure of His power. The attributes of God form the fact and forces which harmonize in the person of God. His infinity, which means there are no bounds, is represented in His attributes. His sovereignty, which means He has all authority or is the rule, is manifested in His decrees. His glory, which involves worship, adoration and praise, is seen in His names. In understanding His persons, we can grasp a hold of the nature of God and understand with better clarity, the meaning of His existence.

2. How can you be sure that there is a God?

We have a fourfold source of knowledge about God. intuition, tradition, reason, and relation. We have been born with an intuitive perception of God which means: that the befile in a personal God is born in every man. The Bible reveals God's character and His person for man and gives a true idea of the divine being. Tradition deals with the early impressions of the race and as that which is present. Adam's testimony concerning God was given directly to the succeeding generation. The present influence of tradition as represented in the instruction of children is the most vital aspect of education. Reason is the third source of the knowledge of God. the logical deductions based on observed realities, the best source to man through nature through manifestation of Himself and His son, and through the scripture. The Bible is absolute truth.

3. How do you define God?

The term "Trinity" is not found in the Bible, the world is delivered from a Latin word meaning "threefold" or "three in one". The Godhead is the trinity in unity, seeing there are there inner distinctions, but a single divine life. "The three persons are equal but one essence". (John 14:11, 16 and 17; John 15:26; 2 Cor. 3:17; Gal. 4:6). The nature of God presents the supreme mystery of our finite minds. The scriptures declare this truth, one essence subsisting in three persons. Human beings are singular in one sense and plural in another; in material and material elements. Therefore it shouldn't be difficult to accept the plurality in the divine exists. The unity of God and the "three in one" God is taught in the old testament as well in the new.

4. How do I talk to God?

The Bible says in Matt. 6:6, "But thou, when thou prayest, enter into the closet, and when thou hast shut thy door, pray to thy father which is in secret; and thy father which seeth in secret shall reward thee openly." This means that prayer is a righteous man availeth much." The way to get through to God in our prayer is through the lord Jesus Christ. For it says in John 14:16, "I am the way, the truth and the life: no man cometh unto the Father, but by me." a righteous man availeth much, the way that we become righteous is through Jesuus Christ, receiving Him as personal Savior, and then God will be able to hear our prayers. Those prayers need to be definite prayers, determined prayers and prayers of dedication. we must talk to God with a total dependence upon His person. To accomplish a clear communication to God, we cannot ask amis according to James 4;2-3. If we ask with wrong motives, if we ask with sin in our heart, if we ask with idols in the heart, we can't really expect any real response from God. Praying simply means communicating with God.

5. Why has God Placed me on earth?

The mystery of man is no mystery at all. The Bible says, "Know ye that the Lord, He is God. it is He that has made us and not we ourselves. We are His people and the sheep of His pasture" (Ps. 100:3). We have a God who is the creator and Lord, and One who decides and manages our destiny. There are only two possible ways to explain the origin of living things: either living things arose by a naturalistic process of evolution or they were created. If one refuses to accept the fact that God exists, the God that created heaven and the earth, then to that person evolution becomes a fact. The reason that most scientists accept the theory of evolution is that they are unbelievers, and unbelieving, materialistic men are forced to accept a materialistic, naturalistic explanation for the origin of all living things. The Bible says, "in the beginning God created" (Gen. 1:1) Man is three-fold. "May the God of peace Himself sanctify you entirely, and may your spirit and soul and body be preserved complete, without blame, at the coming of our Lord Jesus Christ" (1 Thess. 5:23). Man is a spirit because he is dependent upon God. This is the nucleus of life, the life principle, the source of life, God consciousness, worshipful part of man, the likeness of God, the inbreathing of God. "And the Lord God formed man from the dust of the ground and breathed into him the breath of life and man became a living soul" (Gen. 2:7). Man is soul because he has the likeness of God and the body that links him to earth, and God said, "Let us make men in our image, after our likeness" (Gen. 1:26-27). He has personality, individuality, intellect, mind, understanding, sensibility, motion and s body because he possesses flesh, bone, nerve brain, blood and vital organs, "And the Lord God formed man of the dust of the ground" (Gen. 2:7). Chemically man has sixteen elements of soil represented in His body. Six vital minerals are present in organic form and the remaining being water, carbon and glasses. The first man died from the earth (1 Cor. 15:47). Man is created to worship and serve God.

Acknowledgment

I am indebted to the instruction and guidance of my parents to love God. This is how my passion started to study God. I respect the knowledge and loyalty of my professors in residence, extension, and online research studies.

I have high regard for systematic theology by Lewis Sperry Chafer, Th.D Dallas seminary press.

I appreciate the work done with my manuscript by my wife's initial draft and with my granddaughter Jocelyn's final draft. It took patience, scholarship and time. I have gratitude for my congregation, and pastoral health care ministry.

Pastoral Health Care book series

Pastoral health care starts with going beyond ourselves and experiencing the supernatural. The first five books deal with affirming God's essence and compassion, accepting God's endearment and knowledge, adjusting to God's indwelling peace. It includes God;s sufficiency, love, counsel, kingdom, and heart. It is a spiritual source strategy.

The second set of the five books deals with the impartation of divine vitality. The books give us hope and light. It reminds us that through Jesus, we are never alone. You will learn to develop an adequate level of spiritual, Ps.ychological, and physiological adjustments. Learning with confidence will take place. Divine dialogue includes Glorifying God, Dynamic Doer, Satisfying Strength, Discipling Dynamics, and Celebrating Christ. They will place "Above all Christ" in our lives.

The third set of five books deals with supernatural activities. I live an ordinary life abiding in Christ and being an obedient servant of the Lord. I like to dig deeper in God's word (the Bible). Fantastic Favorites includes questions. What does it mean to live in Jesus Christ? What does it mean to live in Jesus Christ? Why do I believe in Jesus Christ? How should I talk to Jesus Christ? Who has brought me to an in depth study of God Jesus Christ.

www.ingramcontent.com/pod-product-compliance
Lightning Source LLC
Chambersburg PA
CBHW061651120626
46550CB00003B/903